Mystery of the Maya

The Golden Age of the Classic Maya

Nancy Ruddell

CANADIAN MUSEUM OF CIVILIZATION

CANADIAN CATALOGUING IN PUBLICATION DATA

Ruddell, Nancy, 1994–

Mystery of the Maya:the golden age of the classic Maya

Issued also in French under the title: Le mystère des Mayas.
Published to complement the IMAX® film *Mystery of the Maya*.

ISBN 0-660-14040-3

1. Mayas. 2. Mayas — Antiquities. 3. Indians of Central
America. 4. Indians of Mexico. I. Canadian Museum of
Civilization. II. Title. III. Title: The golden age of the classic
Maya.

F1435.R82 1995   972.8'1016   C95-980152-9

Published by
Canadian Museum of Civilization
100 Laurier Street
P.O. Box 3100, Station B
Hull, Quebec
J8X 4H2

Drawings:
Douglas Brant Spencer

Editor:
Marcia Rodríguez

Design:
Purich Design Studio

Front cover design:
Yves Paquin

Front cover photograph:
Maya scribe writing in a codex
(reenactment scene from the IMAX® film)

Roll-out photography:
3-D Laser imaging technology developed by the National
Research Council Canada and the Canadian Conservation
Institute. (See pages 14, 17, 20, and 22.)

*Thanks to Mario Pérez Campa of the Instituto nacional de
antropología y historia for his valuable comments.*

Canada

Contents

Introduction

Tremendous progress has been made in unravelling the mysteries of the Maya civilization since their ancient ruins first caught world attention over a century ago. Thanks to the work of archaeologists, linguists, and contemporary Maya, we have learned a great deal about Maya social, political, and religious practices. Those living in the vicinity of the ruins have always known of these abandoned cities — they continue to visit the temples, still performing their religious rituals.

The Imax® film, *Mystery of the Maya*, is an opportunity to see these spectacular sites and marvel at the genius of the people who built them. This book complements the film by providing a glimpse into the history and worldview of the Maya. The evolution of their culture is a lesson in adaptation and survival. In learning about the Maya past, we can gain insight into how cultures maintain their integrity in the face of hardships and changing circumstances.

The ruins at Palenque, photographed in 1890 by Alfred Maudslay

Courtesy of the Brooklyn Museum Library Collection

Chapter One

Maya Civilization

A Bonampak king holding a spear decorated with jaguar skins. He wears a jaguar-skin tunic, a jade-effigy breast plate, and an elaborate feather headdress.

AN OVERVIEW

The remarkable achievements of the Maya equal those of the Egyptians, the Chinese, and the Greeks. This culture, which began evolving over 4,000 years ago, developed into highly structured kingdoms during the Classic period, A.D. 250–900. Their complex society consisted of many independent states, each with a rural farming community and large urban sites built around civic centres with plazas, temples, and monuments. The Maya perfected a writing system that recorded their beliefs and historical events, used sophisticated mathematics for their calendars and astronomy, and built massive structures strategically placed to reflect their sense of cosmic order.

Maya writings document some of the major changes that took place as their culture evolved from small farming communities into numerous urban societies. The first shift occurred around 300 B.C., when rule by nobles and kings became a norm in Maya society. Another significant change was the mysterious abandonment by the southern Maya of their cities around A.D. 900. The northern Maya moved into a new phase as they came under the influence of their Toltec neighbours and other groups that settled in the Yucatán Peninsula. This era continued until the arrival of the Spanish in 1541, which ushered in a dark period that witnessed Maya books burned and attempts made to obliterate the Maya religion.

Maya history can be characterized as cycles of rise and fall: city-states rose in prominence and fell into decline, only to be replaced by others. It could also be described as one of continuity and change, guided by a religion that remains the foundation of their culture. For those who follow ancient Maya traditions, the

Map of Mesoamerica today

Map of Mesoamerica, Classic period: A.D. *250–900*

belief in the influence of the cosmos on human lives and the necessity of paying homage to the gods through rituals continues to find expression in a modern hybrid Christian-Maya faith.

As in the past, maize (corn) is one of the cornerstones of their culture. It is their staple food, providing sustenance and bringing spiritual significance to their daily lives. Maya-speaking people still live in their ancient homeland where they raise corn and weave beautiful cotton fabrics imbued with symbolic meaning.

Their survival has once again been threatened in recent times. While many Maya people have been killed during civil wars, others from countries such as Guatemala have been forced to flee their homes and seek refuge in countries such as Mexico, the United States, and Canada. Human-rights groups are calling for an end to these injustices and governments are working to find lasting solutions to the problems of discrimination and cultural genocide.

THE MAYA HOMELAND

Today close to 6 million Maya live in their ancestral homeland, which spans five countries of the ancient region known as Mesoamerica — Mexico, Guatemala, Belize, Honduras, and El Salvador. One of the most varied environments on earth, it ranges from the lowlands of the Yucatán Peninsula to the mountain highlands along the Pacific Ocean. The climate is hot and humid with a rainy and a dry season.

The volcanic mountain region to the west yielded such desirable products as the highly prized obsidian (volcanic glass), grinding stones for processing maize, jade for making ornaments worn by nobles, and the sacred quetzal bird's brilliant green feathers, which graced the headdresses of kings. In addition, the rich volcanic soil on the mountain sides has been terraced for maize growing over the centuries.

The ancient cities of the Classic period developed in the Petén southern lowlands. A large variety of animals lived in the tropical rain forest, including deer, rabbits, armadilloes, and the feared jaguar (hunted for its pelt), a symbol of kingly power and prestige. The northern lowlands of the Yucatán consist of a giant limestone shelf with a thin layer of soil to support the forest growth. As there are few lakes, a system of irrigation dykes and canals was built to contain the water for urban needs and probably for growing corn. Water was also available from deep natural wells and large water holes called *cenotes*. The rainy season lasted from May through early November, when all efforts were directed to the cornfields to ensure the food supply for the coming year.[1]

A warrior holding a spear and wearing a short-sleeved battle jacket. The head of a captive is attached to his waist.

THE OLMEC: 1200–100 B.C.

Maya culture traces its roots to the Olmec kingdom, a domain that spanned the swampy southernmost arc of the Gulf of Mexico. The people were called Olmeca, "people of the rubber[-tree] country," because they lived in an area known for its rubber trees. First appearing on the scene about 3,000 years ago, they developed an artistic style and a spiritual concept of the universe that united the different groups throughout Mesoamerica into a single cultural entity.[2] The Olmec worldview influenced the Maya when they began building cities with ceremonial centres.

Who were the Olmec and where did they come from? Although there is no definitive answer to these questions, clues about what they looked like can be gleaned from their stone sculptures, terracotta figures, and ceremonial jade objects. Images carved on stone monuments show tall, muscular leaders. Huge sculptured stone heads ranging from 1.5 to 4 metres high, the largest of which has been estimated at sixty-five tons, may be depictions of their kings.[3] Images of men emerging from caves wearing helmets and carrying tools suggest that the Olmec were a highly developed society.

The Olmec developed new ideas and possessed knowledge that profoundly influenced Maya culture. For example, they recorded information using an early form of hieroglyphic writing, developed a counting system using dots and bars, and probably initiated the development of the Long Count calendar that put their year one at 3114 B.C. in our modern (Gregorian) calendar. They carved jade and stone figures of the were-jaguar, the first depiction of a god known in this part of the world. His features, which combine those of a snarling jaguar and a weeping child, suggest an early form of rain god.[4] The Olmec also built ceremonial centres keyed to a celestial orientation and produced precious effigies from jade and other semi-precious stones. Their architecture required a high level of stone-working and engineering skills that had no precedent in the New World. All of these elements became part of the Maya culture. The Olmec civilization at its height (near the end of the Middle Preclassic period, 900–300 B.C.) occupied at least forty urban sites. Their influence spread west and

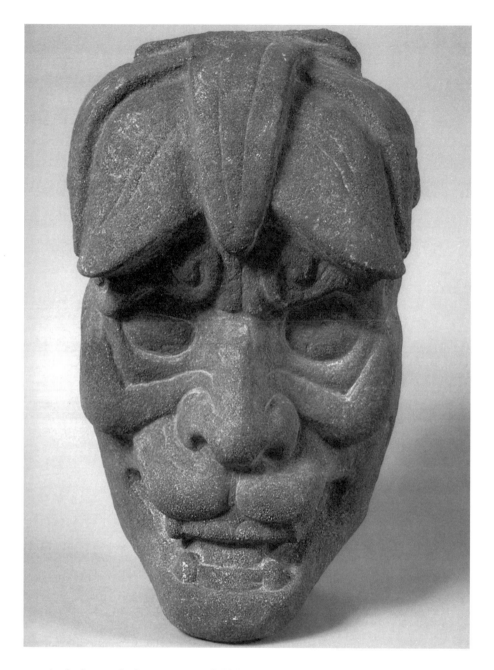

A Were-jaguar God mask representing the God of Rain and Lightning (replica)

Photo: Harry Foster
(CMC S95-24,284)

particularly south, leaving an indelible mark on all the indigenous populations of Mesoamerica.

For unknown reasons, the Olmec disappeared around 600 B.C. As they left their cities, they attempted to bury their colossal stone heads, some of which have been found toppled from their bases and others mutilated with large holes punched into the stone. The Olmec may have deliberately damaged these sculptures as part of a ritual to neutralize the power held in them since they were no longer needed.[5]

Chapter Two

The Beginnings of Maya Culture[6]

EARLY PRECLASSIC PERIOD: 1800–900 B.C.

The first people to occupy the Yucatán Peninsula were hunters and gathers who arrived some 11,000 years ago. These nomadic people lived in small family bands, hunting game using chipped stone tools fashioned into knives, scrapers, and projectile points. Around 2500 B.C. they started cultivating maize and abandoned a nomadic way of life to settle in villages surrounded by cornfields.

The Maya created arable land by using a "slash-and-burn" technique to clear the forests. They planted maize and secondary crops such as beans, squash, and tobacco. In the highlands to the west, they terraced the slopes on mountainsides; in the low-

Village scene at the cenote, Dzibilchaltún, with thatched-roof huts in the background (reenactment scene from the IMAX® film)

lands, they cleared the jungle for planting. After a period of two years,[7] they moved their fields to new locations, allowing the old fields to lie fallow for ten years before reusing them.

They lived in small villages consisting of household compounds occupied by extended families. Their thatched-roof houses were usually one-room huts with walls of interwoven wooden poles covered with dried mud. These huts were used primarily for sleeping while daily chores such as cooking took place outdoors in the central communal compound. The division of labour between men and

"Shield Jaguar" accepting a water-lily helmet from his principal wife, Lady Xoc (from a Yaxchilán stone lintel)

women was clearly defined: the men looked after building huts and caring for the cornfields and the women prepared food, made clothing, and tended to the family's domestic needs. These ancient farming methods and family traditions have persisted over the centuries and continue to be followed in many rural communities today.

MIDDLE PRECLASSIC PERIOD: 900–300 B.C.

By the Middle Preclassic period, Olmec beliefs and ideas about hierarchical methods of organizing society had probably infiltrated the Maya population. The southern Maya in the mountain valleys of present-day western Honduras, Guatemala, and El Salvador showed strong evidence of Olmec influence — they began raising ceremonial mounds with plazas, carving stone monuments, and displaying images depicting symbols of gods and kings. Although the people to the west and south of the southern lowland region chose to unite under high-ranking chiefs or kings, most of the lowland Maya resisted the pres-

sure to conform and continued to maintain an egalitarian model of government, preferring tribal confederacies that recognized no power above their village patriarchs.

LATE PRECLASSIC PERIOD: 300 B.C.–A.D. 250

The Late Preclassic period witnessed the emergence of the *ahau*, or high king, and the rise of kingdoms throughout Maya lands. By the first century B.C., the concept of kings as patriarchal heads of extended families was accepted in the majority of lowland states. The kings viewed themselves as brothers, since they were all descendants of the same ancestors who began their lineages in the distant past. For the first time, the Maya recorded the history of their kings: the lowland people decorated their temples and the highland people erected stone monuments carved with glyphs and narrative pictures describing their rituals. This practice set the stage for the next thousand years, during which the principles of kingship dominated Maya life.

Chapter Three

The Golden Era

CLASSIC PERIOD:
A.D. 250–900
During this period, known as the golden era, the population of the Maya has been estimated at several million, with the main sphere of activity in the southern lowlands of the Yucatán. When the southern states collapsed around A.D. 900, the centre of power shifted to the northern Yucatán states. At its height, the southern lowland region boasted as many as sixty different kingdoms each ruled by a king.

THE SOUTHERN LOWLAND CITIES
The Aztec city of Teotihuacán, founded around 100 B.C., was the first major metropolis to develop in Mesoamerica. For centuries, Teotihuacán

Tikal's Great Plaza with the Temple of the Giant Jaguar on the right

was the cultural, religious, and trading centre of Mesoamerica.8 At its zenith, its population swelled to approximately 200,000 people, but its greatness faded around A.D. 700, perhaps because of political turmoil and crop failures. Cerros was one of the early Maya cities to embrace the concept of kingship and build a complex of temples and ball courts starting around 50 B.C. A hundred years later, the city was abandoned. The inhabitants gave up their kings and returned to farming and fishing.

(1)  (2) 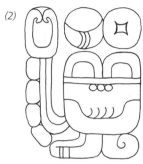 (3)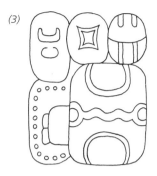

Emblems for the cities of Tikal (1), Yaxchilán (2), and Palenque (3)

Tikal was another Maya centre that grew into a city about the same time as Cerros. By A.D. 600, Tikal had surpassed Teotihuacán to become the largest Maya city-state, boasting 50,000 inhabitants. Located in the heart of the Petén jungle, its sprawling ruins of over 10 kilometres include lofty temples, and massive palaces. Thousands of thatch-roofed hut compounds would have lined the streets and pathways in all directions around these structures. Other smaller centres under Tikal's rule varied between populations of 5,000 to 10,000. By A.D. 869, the last stone carving was set in Tikal's Great Plaza, and thirty years later the city was abandoned. The succession of kings has not been forgotten, however : their history is carved in stone. With the deciphering of Maya hieroglyphics, we can now identify their names and birthdates, when they ascended to the throne, the rituals they performed, and the time of their death.

Besides Tikal, a number of other cities played a prominent role in the southern lowlands during the late Classic period (A.D. 600–900). Yaxchilán controlled the central region; Palenque dominated the southwestern region; Calakmul controlled the southern Yucatán peninsula; and Copán became the primary centre in the southeast.[9] They remained independent city-states, trading with each other and sharing the common traits of Maya culture.

THE FIRST KINGS

Within each Maya kingdom, society was organized hierarchically, including kings, nobles, teachers, scribes, warriors, architects, engineers, professionals, administrators, craftsmen, merchants, traders, labourers, and farmers. Each state was ruled by a high king who used the title *ahau*. Besides the capital, outlying subsidiary sites ranged from sizeable towns down to hamlets and extended-family farming compounds. The smaller centres came under the control of a lesser-ranking noble who was often related to the king.

Ruling was no easy task. The king's duties were many: coping with political

The Labná arch is the finest example of a Maya portal arch. It was constructed from two sets of nine stones with a single flat stone at the top. The nine stones represent the nine levels of the Underworld.

Men preparing to transport terracotta pots used to store food and water (reenactment scene from the IMAX® film)

complexities in maintaining control over his domain; expanding his territory as far as possible; organizing military offensives and defending his territory against threats from neighbouring states; proving his legitimate right to rule while remaining wary of rivals from within the noble class who could challenge his position. It was his responsibility to negotiate trading alliances, maintain the business of the court and the state, and undertake municipal and architectural projects. With the help of his advisors, he determined when to go to war, knowing he could be captured and killed as a sacrifice to the gods. One of his prime roles, beyond civic duties, was to intercede with the spirit world, bringing divine energy into the material world to guide his people and ensure the success of their endeavours.

EXPANDING THE CORNFIELDS

There may be several reasons why the Maya moved away from the small farming communities ruled by local officials to the complex kingdoms of the Classic period. Finding ways to collect rainwater and creating more arable land for agriculture were two important developments that played a major role in bringing about these changes. These innovations set the stage for increased food production, enhanced trade with neighbouring states, and subsequent population growth. The need for a government to administer the intricacies of expanded urban and rural activities may in part explain why the Maya adopted the king as head of state.

To solve the problem of drought during the dry season, reservoirs and cisterns were excavated. Rainwater was channelled off buildings and streets into these reservoirs during the rainy season. In the lowlands of the Yucatán, a massive system of canals was constructed to drain the swamps, exposing the highly fertile soil to be converted into cornfields. To get around the problem of soil depletion, the raised swampland fields were fertilized by placing sediment and aquatic plants collected from the canals onto the soil. This created a self-sustaining ecosystem that ensured the production of corn beyond the needs of the local population.

As a result of this expanded economic activity, a bureaucracy was developed to manage state affairs. A sizeable labour force was organized to build and maintain the waterworks and tend the cornfields. The quantities of corn produced created a surplus, available as a principal trade commodity. With increased trade came more wealth and the growth of cities into large city-states that evolved into a highly sophisticated civilization.

COLLAPSE OF THE MAYA CITIES[10]

The Classic period ended around A.D. 900 with the collapse of the southern lowland cities. The northern Yucatán cities, the largest being Chichén Itzá, continued to thrive until they too were abandoned around A.D. 1200, left to be reclaimed by the jungle.

No one knows for sure why these magnificent cities were left to ruin. The reasons are probably numerous and complex. A growing population, drought, and crop failure may have led to serious food shortages and malnutrition. More and more arable land was taken up by growing cities that continued to swell in size,

King "Bird Jaguar" capturing an enemy named "Jewelled Skull"

partly owing to the influx of people arriving from outside the region. When crops failed, people may have been forced to move elsewhere to survive. The escalation of hostilities later in the period, the distaste for increased warfare, and the practice of taking commoners for human sacrifice may have been other factors (in the Early Classic period, only kings and captured nobles were used as human sacrifices).

People may have grown weary of supporting the high price of war and maintaining the concept of kingship. The cost of keeping a growing number of nobles, and the expense of building an increasing number of higher and more elaborate temples may have become more than society could bear. Whatever the reasons, the Maya decided to give up their kings and cities and return to a simpler form of life as farmers of maize — living in rural villages much as they do today.

Figurine of a noblewoman with tattooed cheeks and a step-cut hairstyle popular in the Classic period

Photo: Harry Foster (CMC S95-24,292)

Chapter Four

Maya Religion

THE MAYA SACRED BOOK: THE *POPOL VUH*[11]

The *Popol Vuh* is contained in a sixteenth-century manuscript that preserves the sacred and secular history of the Quiché Maya of Guatemala. The text reveals patterns of cosmic order and defines Maya understanding of the forces in the universe that directly influenced their lives. Because most of the ancient Maya codices have not survived (they were either burned by the Spanish or lost to the ravages of time), it is fortunate that some sixteenth-century Quiché lords learned to write their language using the Roman alphabet. In the *Popol Vuh* they left an invaluable legacy that describes the accomplishments and beliefs of a civilization stretching back into antiquity. One of the most important texts included in this epic is the creation story, which laid the foundation of Maya thought.

THE CREATION STORY: AN INTRODUCTION

The creation story is key to understanding the basic assumptions underlying Maya religion, art, and literature. The eloquent opening of this book describes creation as beginning with the utterance of a word and the appearance of the thing embodied by the word.[12] The Maya believe that the material world is imbued with spiritual energy from which it was conceived. Their creation story tells how the universe came into being, the struggle between the light and the dark in overcoming death, and how humans must fulfil their responsibility towards the earth and the heavens. The principles of the myth have guided the evolution of Maya culture for thousands of years and continue to be of vital importance to contemporary Maya.

The Maya believe the world was created and destroyed four times before humans made an appearance.[13] After the third creation, a great flood occurred and the sky fell to earth. To hold up the sky, gods were placed at the earth's four corners. After three unsuccessful attempts to make humans from mud, wood, and flesh, the Maker finally succeeded in creating sentient beings by combining ground maize with water to form maize dough.[14] This fourth and present cycle of creation began on 13 August 3114 B.C.

THE FIRST TWO CREATIONS

The Creator Couple, also known as the Maker, Modeller, Sovereign Plumed Serpent, and the Heart of the Sea, were responsible for the first and all subsequent creations. In the beginning, there was only the sky lying directly on top of the calm primordial sea. The Creator Couple, the embodiment of both male and female, began by stretching a cord to create the four corners of the sky-earth.

In the second creation, the Creator Couple came together to devise a plan to fashion the universe.[15] They began by planting three stones of the heavenly hearth, raising the sky, and emptying the water to form the earth's own platform. At their command, the earth rose up and the mountains, lakes, and forests appeared. They then created all the creatures of the earth — animals, birds, and insects. But the Makers were discontent because they had not made their ideal: creatures who could speak, pray, and keep track of time, beings who could reciprocate their love and care by returning nourishment to them.[16] As their attempts to make humans proved unsuccessful, they ordered a great flood to destroy the earth so that they could begin their third attempt at creation.

THE THIRD CREATION: THE HERO TWINS

The third creation is the world of the Hero Twins. Their father and uncle, who were also twins, were known as great ball players. The noise of their bouncing ball disturbed the Lords of Death, who lived just below the ball court floor in Xibalbá (Place of Fright), the Maya Underworld. They summoned the players to answer for their misdemeanours, and after a series of trials, the ball players were killed and their bodies buried under the floor of the ball court. The Lords severed the head of the Hero Twins' father and placed it in a tree as a warning to others. One day a curious young Xibalban girl went to see the skull, who asked her to hold open her hand. The skull spit on her hand and impregnated her. Her father was furious, so she was banished to the Middle World of humans and found shelter with her babies' grandmother. Her name is Lady Blood and she called her twins Hunahpu and Xbalanque.

The boys' adventures included catching a rat who had stolen seeds from the cornfields. To purchase his freedom, he told the twins where they could find their father's and uncle's ball game equipment. They immediately started playing, making such a racket that they disturbed the Lords of Death. The twins were summoned to Xibalbá, where they were put through a number of tests. They were smarter then their father and uncle, however, and were able to outwit the Lords of Death. Each day they played the ball game against the Lords of Death to a scoreless tie. Each night they outsmarted the Xibalbans in trials meant to kill the twins. One night they demonstrated their

The Hero Twins

Hero Twin Hunahpu shooting the Celestial Bird with a blowgun

power by jumping into an oven of raging fire and then coming back to life five days later. Finally, in a command performance before the Lords of Death, they tempted the Lords into allowing themselves to be sacrificed, and when they were dead, the twins did not revive them. Thus, they banished the Xibalbans from the world of humans.[17] The twins then went to the ball court to resurrect their father and uncle (who represent different forms of the Maize God).

The final event in the third creation took place when the twins confronted the Celestial Bird, Seven Macaw, a beautiful but vain creature who declared himself to be the sun and commanded everyone to worship him. The twins decided to teach Seven Macaw and his sons a lesson and shot him with a pellet from their blowgun. The pellet struck his tooth and caused great pain. In desperation, he asked his grandfather for help, who said he would have to remove Seven Macaw's teeth and eyes. When he did this, everyone saw Seven Macaw for what he was and his greatness left him. His sons continued to make mischief: they lured four hundred boys into their house and then collapsed the roof, killing all of them.

When the twins rose from Xibalbá, one became the sun and the other the moon. The boys who were killed rose with them and became stars.

THE FOURTH CREATION: THE FIRST HUMANS

The Hero Twins set the scene for the fourth creation, the one we are now living in. The Creator Couple spoke: "The dawn has approached and morning has come for humankind — born in the light, begotten in the light." They knew that true people would be made from yellow and white corn. From the cleft opening at the sacred Split-Mountain, the First Mother fashioned the first human beings from maize dough and water. She ground the corn nine times and it became human flesh; the grease from the water in which she washed her hands became human fat. These humans were perfect beings and knew everything. They turned to their Creators and thanked them. The humans could see as well as the gods — all the way to the four sides of creation. Although the Creators were pleased, they decided to change them just a little. They were troubled because the newly created humans could see

Vessel depicting a nobleman offering bread (made from multilayered dough, including maize) to the gods

Photo: Harry Foster
(CMC S95-24,287)

Roll-out photo: (CMC K95-443)

everywhere, through the earth and sky to the limits of the universe. Since humans were now like gods, the Creators decided to blur their vision so they could see clearly only those things close to them.[18] In this way, humanity was given permanent myopia.

Chapter Five

The Symbolic Meaning of the Creation Story

MAIZE DOUGH AND THE THREE STONES

Like all genesis myths, the Maya creation myth is symbolic. For example, maize dough is equated with human flesh and the original waters of creation with human blood. Through the ritual giving of alms or sustenance, called *k'awil* in the Maya language, people give back to the gods what the deities gave people in the first place — maize and water transformed into flesh and blood. The central role of food offerings, meals, and ceremonial banquets in Maya religious life hinges on this equation.[19]

The three stones used in the creation of the cosmic hearth found at the centre of the world are symbolized by the stones used to surround the central cooking fire in Maya homes. Like these stones that centred the cosmos and allowed the sky to be lifted from the primordial sea, the central hearth symbolizes an altar from which smoke rises carrying prayers and messages to the Sky World. In the first creation, the Creator Couple used a measuring cord that stretched up to the sky from the central hearth and reached down to the four corners of the earth, delineating the sacred cardinal directions. Each of the four

K'awil God

Quetzal Bird

directions has a special tree, bird, colour, and god associated with it. For example, east (where the sun is born) is red; west (where the sun falls back into the dark Underworld) is black; north (home of the cooling rains and the North Star around which the sky pivots) is white; south (considered the sun's right hand) is yellow.[20]

The Maya believe the world is alive with spiritual energy. The directional patterns of the four corners of the world were established by the gods. When the Maya built their cities around ceremonial centres, they aligned the buildings with the cardinal compass points to establish sacred landscapes on earth. For example, the temples around the central plazas were built in a matrix grid aligned north-south and east-west. In so doing, humans created order in the physical world that complements god-generated patterns in the spiritual realm. Their world was made to mirror the spiritual dimension, the one humans normally cannot see because of their limited vision.

THE THREE DIMENSIONS OF THE MAYA WORLD

Maya visualize the earth as a horizontal plane that intersects with the Sky World and the Underworld. A ceiba or silk-cotton tree grows at the earth's centre where the first three stones were placed and the sacred mountain rose. This Great Tree, the central pole that holds up the sky, symbolizes the *axis mundi*, an invisible line that joins the three worlds. Its branches reach into the Upper World, its roots grow deep into the Underworld, and its trunk spans the Middle World. Souls travelled up and down this sacred tree, which is sometimes depicted as a maize plant or an elaborately decorated cross.

The earth is envisioned as a living being, a turtle floating on a vast sea. When humans die, they fall through a cleft or crack in the turtle's back into the Underworld, a dark, forbidding place associated with misery and pestilence, which the average human cannot escape. Each day the sun rises from the East Door and travels across the sky to fall through the West Door into the Underworld, creating night and day. When the sun rises again in the east, the miracle of rebirth begins, and people are assured that their prayers for the continuance of life have been heard.

MAYA GODS

The many Maya gods were considered *ch'u* or holy beings. They were either sky gods, earth gods, or gods of the Underworld. In the Classic Maya texts and in the *Popol Vuh*, creation was seen as the result of a great effort by many gods who each had a role to play in the unfolding of the universe. These gods are depicted on terracotta plates, cups, vessels, and plaster walls, and in stone carvings found on monuments and public buildings. There are many variations on the creation story and on the way the gods are named and portrayed in Maya art. A description of a few of the principal gods can be found in Appendix A.

Vessel depicting a dancing snake-man representing death and the Underworld

Photo: Harry Foster
(CMC S95-24,289)

Roll-out photo:
(CMC K95-442)

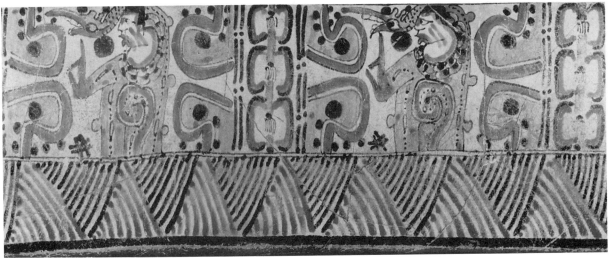

Chapter Six

Royal Duties

COMMUNICATIONS WITH THE GODS

Kings played an important role in contacting the gods and ancestors. The king was considered the living embodiment of a god, an incarnation of the central Great Tree or world axis (the same as in the creation story) along which divine energy enters the material world.[21] In fact, kings are sometimes depicted wearing headdresses that evoke an image of a tree.

As throngs of citizens watched from the plaza below, kings and nobles conducted ritual ceremonies on the platforms of temples, which were also used as royal tombs, and were often built around hills or mountains. Over the centuries, kings constructed their temples on top of existing ones, with the oldest in the centre and subsequent ones layered like the skin of an onion. As a result, the buildings grew taller and wider, gradually reaching higher and higher towards the heavens. These structures, which symbolize *witz*, the First Mountain of the creation story, were erected at sacred sites that have a concentration of spiritual energy.

Some temple façades are ornamented with masks of beings such as the First Mountain, the rising and setting sun gods, the Vision Serpent, and other cosmic monsters. The Vision Serpent

Stone mask on a temple at Copán

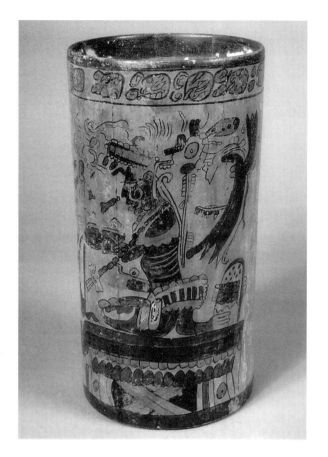

mask represents the communion between earth and sky, the mask's wide-open mouth symbolizing the door kings took when they were transported into the spirit world. On temple platforms and in specially designated buildings, kings conducted ritual bloodletting ceremonies and sacred dance performances. Courts and plazas were the settings for great pageants that enabled nobles to travel to the spirit world where power and wisdom was bestowed upon them.[22]

BLOODLETTING RITUALS

During the Classic period, kings, their wives, and members of the elite performed bloodletting rituals publicly and in the privacy of their homes. They believed that one of their principal duties was to provide sustenance for the gods. A king used an obsidian knife or a stingray spine to cut his penis, allowing the blood to fall onto paper held in a bowl. Kings' wives also took part in this ritual by pulling a rope with thorns attached through their tongues. The blood-stained paper was burned, the rising smoke directly communicating with the Upper World and fulfilling humanity's duty to nurture the gods. In modern

Terracotta vessel depicting a king performing a bloodletting ritual and bringing divine energy (itz) *back into the world*
Photo: Harry Foster (CMC S95-24,286) Roll-out photo: (CMC K95-445)

Royal women from Bonampak performing a bloodletting ritual. The woman on the right pierces her tongue to let the blood drip onto the paper in the bowl; the woman on the left pulls a cord with thorns through her tongue.

times, this ritual is carried out by sacrificing chickens or turkeys. For the Maya, blood sacrifice was necessary for the survival of both gods and people, sending human energy skyward and receiving divine power in return.[23]

During the bloodletting ceremonies, Maya kings went into a trance induced by the loss of blood and the use of hallucinogenic drugs. The trance transported them into the spirit world and allowed them to obtain knowledge about the fate of their people, a fate that, according to Maya belief, was directed by the gods. Each time kings penetrated the membrane separating the physical and spiritual worlds, they were breaking down barriers between humans and the gods.

Other sacred matter such as copal (a type of incense), maize dough, and rubber was burned in huge fires, transforming the souls contained in these substances into smoke. As in the bloodletting rituals, this smoke rose to the Sky World as food for the gods.

PUBLIC PERFORMANCES

Public performances of ritual dancing and dramas, in which kings and nobles were transformed into gods by entering a visionary trance, were another means of communication with the spirit world. There were more than twenty major ceremonies throughout the solar year, including reenactments of the creation story and other important cosmic events. Marked by singing, the playing of musical instruments — trumpets, rattles, flutes, drums, and whistles — and the shouts and jeers of thousands who came to witness the event, these rituals reaffirmed the king's power to act as a vessel in bringing supernatural powers into his domain for the benefit of his people.[24]

Terracotta vessel depicting dancing noblemen
Photo: Harry Foster (CMC S95-24,285) Roll-out photo: (CMC K95-444)

Ball Players

THE BALL GAME

The ball game was first played by the Hero Twins and their father and uncle in the creation story. Introduced by the Olmec, this game was later adopted by the Maya, who built over four hundred playing courts in their cities. The courts were shaped like the capital letter **I**, with slanting side walls and a floor the size of a tennis court. Commoners played various types of ball games for sport, but only captured kings, nobles, and lords played the ritual war game. The game would have been played at designated times according to the dictates of the sacred 260-day calendar.

Each team consisted of seven players who propelled a large solid rubber ball off their hips, elbows, and thighs, from one side of the court to the other. They were not allowed to touch the ball with their hands or legs. To protect their bodies, the players wore gloves and leather or cotton padding around the pelvis, legs, and forearms.

A stone object like a gorget or pendant hung from the neck. Gear included headdresses and symbols of important gods, which elevated their play to the level of a great cosmic drama. It is unclear whether the headdresses and other symbolic regalia were worn during the game, or reserved for postgame ceremonies. Players were probably dressed only in their protective clothing, as they needed to be extremely quick and agile in order to return the ball with the necessary velocity.[25]

Although the rules of the ball game have not survived, a sixteenth-century account describes how points were scored in northern cities such as Chichén Itzá. A point was made when the ball was driven through a ring on the side of the court or when the ball hit the floor on the opponents' side. When the game ended, the captain of the losing team was put to death as a ritual sacrifice to the gods. He would then be reborn into the Sky World. This ceremony symbolized the original sacrifice and resurrection of the Maize God.

The ball game is symbolic of the life-and-death battle that took place during the third creation. The floor of the court represents the earth's platform, which separates the human world from the Underworld. For centuries, commoners buried their dead under the dirt floor of their huts, just as the Hero Twins' father and uncle were buried under the ball court floor in the creation story. It was the gods who determined the winners of the ball game, just as they decided who would be victorious at war.

Chapter Seven

Kings and Their Symbols

PACAL: A GREAT KING[26]

In 1952, the tomb of King Pacal at Palenque's famous Temple of Inscriptions was opened for the first time since his funeral in A.D. 683. The rubble that blocked access to the long narrow staircase leading to the burial chamber had finally been cleared. Pacal was eighty years old when he died. His reign, and that of his son, Chan-Bahlum, are credited with inspiring and nurturing the exceptional beauty of Palenque's art and architecture. The building he commissioned as his temple-tomb and the sarcophagus that would hold his body are testimony to the genius of this man.

Moving the sarcophagus lid from Pacal's tomb (reenactment scene from the IMAX® film)

The carved limestone sarcophagus lid depicts Pacal at the moment of his death. Shown falling down the World Tree into the jaws of the Underworld, he is accompanied by the head of a skeletal monster carrying a bowl marked with the glyph of the sun. This is a symbol of reincarnation — like the sun that circles the Underworld to be reborn into the Sky World, Pacal will be reborn as a god who ascends to the heavens. As king, he is the living manifestation of the Hero Twins, who overcame death by defeating the Lords of the Underworld.

Pacal at the moment of his death, falling down the World Tree into the Underworld
Drawing by Merle Greene Robertson

Pacal's mother, Lady Zac, emerging from the Underworld

Portraits of his mother, Lady Zac-Kuk, his great-grandmother, Lady Kanal-Ikal, his father, Kan-Bahlum-Mo, and other ancestors can be seen around the four sides of the coffin. Each figure is being reborn by emerging from a crack in the earth, and wears a headdress symbolizing a fruit tree. Hieroglyphs around the edge of the lid list the deaths of previous kings. The lid has been estimated at as much as five tons and the sarcophagus itself in excess of fifteen tons. Because of its enormous weight and size, it was set in place before the temple construction began.

Maya kings normally inherited the title through their fathers. Pacal's father was not a king, but his mother and great-grandmother were both powerful women who ruled as true kings. Although this created a dilemma for the government because of the convention of patrilineal descent, these two exceptional women defied tradition. Pacal established an unshakeable claim to the throne through them, and explained this change as preordained by the gods.

To legitimize his claim, he declared his mother to be the living embodiment of the First Mother, who created the gods and humans. It followed that Pacal was the son of a goddess. To add more weight to his argument, he maintained that his birthdate and that of the First Mother were the same, thereby securing his rightful position as king.

SYMBOLS OF ROYALTY

Maya kings wore ornate ceremonial clothing and carried sceptres that identified them as sovereign divine rulers. Their regalia linked them to the creation story and to the power of the gods, and was designed to convince subjects of their ability to intercede with the spirit world and guide the affairs of the people.

Kings wore a variety of elaborate headdresses depicting different gods and cosmic monsters. Some headdresses, for example, were made from maize leaves, associated with the Maize God; others were shaped like a tree, symbolic of the Great Tree; still others incorporated a bird image or the brilliant green feathers of the sacred quetzal bird, a link with Itzam-Yeh in the creation story. Other deities frequently represented include the Jester God and the God of Sustenance, both symbols of royalty.

Jewellery was another distinguishing feature of kingly dress. Jade necklaces, headbands, pendants, rings, and earplugs were all signs of noble birth. Kings also wore belts with different ritual items hanging from them such as carved jade images of gods, celts (chisel-shaped axes), and trophy heads of sacrificial victims. They sometimes draped loincloths over their belts, which were decorated with a variety of images of snakes, deities, and warrior symbols, or with weaving patterns that represent the fashioning of human fate. These same patterns are often seen on the sides of temples. Another important emblem for kings was the water lily, the beautiful flower that nourished the cornfields and provided sustenance for the continuation of life.

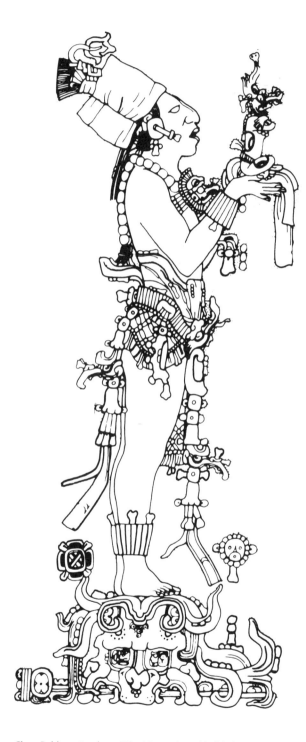

Chan-Bahlum stands on Witz Mountain and holds the Jester God. Drawing by Linda Schele

Royal symbols: jaguar playing with a water lily

The Celestial Bird landing on the foliated Cross, symbol of the World Tree

Drawing by Linda Schele

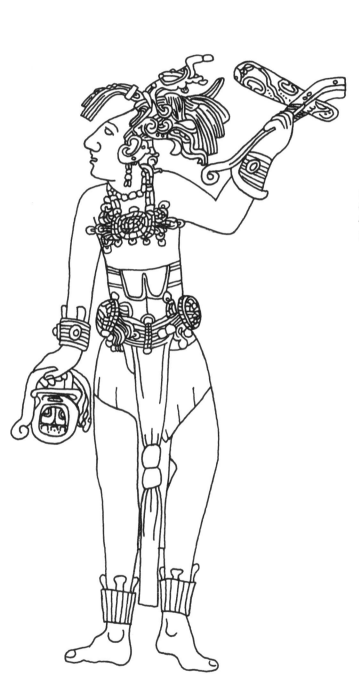

A ruler impersonating Chac, the Rain God, with one foot raised in the dancing position. He holds an axe (or flint) with lightning marks on the blade in one hand and a serpent in the other.

To demonstrate their prowess, kings are pictured holding axes (flints) and weapons of war such as spears, spear throwers, clubs, and shields. They wore jaguar skins to indicate their power as warriors; to demonstrate success at war, they are shown surrounded by human captives with bound hands, usually men of noble birth who were killed as blood sacrifices to the gods.

Perhaps the two most important symbols associated with royalty are the Great Tree and the Serpent Bar,[27] both of which relate to the king's role as the living embodiment of the world axis, the Great Tree. Kings often had themselves portrayed on the Great Tree, as on Pacal's tomb, for example. These trees are also drawn in the shape of an elaborate foliated cross with a horizontal crossbeam that represents a Serpent Bar.

Many images show kings holding serpent-shaped sceptres. These rods appear in various forms, such as a serpent-footed axe, the double-headed Serpent Bar, or the Vision Snake. By holding a serpent rod, kings grasp the path that leads to the spirit world as it is the serpent who opens the way for the king to travel into another dimension. The double-headed Serpent Bar is sometimes depicted with god-heads emerging from the two ends of the rod, a demonstration of the king's ability to materialize gods in the human world.

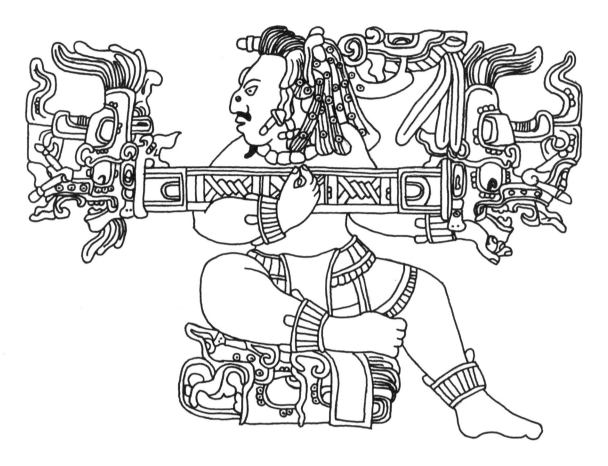

Ah-Zacol, a ruling nobleman of the Kingdom of Bonampak, holding a double-headed bar depicting the K'awil God

Chapter Eight

Maya Sciences

MAYA ASTRONOMY

Maya astronomers looked to the heavens for guidance. They used observatories to trace and calculate the complex motions of the sun, the stars, and planets, and recorded this information in their chronicles, or codices. From these observations, the Maya developed calendars to keep track of celestial movements and the passage of time. In their cities, ceremonial centres designed by highly skilled engineers and architects were aligned with precise compass orien-

Maya astronomers
Drawing by Michael Closs

tations. At the spring and fall equinoxes, the sun cast its rays through small openings in the observatories, lighting up interior walls. Tikal's stone zodiac calendar may have once hung in such a way, to be illuminated twice a year as the sun penetrated the heart of the temple. The most famous example of alignment can be observed at Chichén Itzá, the principal sacred city of the Yucatán. Here people still gather each year, as they have for centuries past, to observe the sun illuminating the stairs of the temple dedicated to the Feathered Serpent God. At the two equinoxes, the sun hits the stairs and the serpent head at its base, creating an image of a luminous snake descending from the sacred mountain to earth.

Why did the Maya go to such lengths to align their ceremonial plazas and temples with the sun and stars and create calendars based on astronomical observations? Although calendars keep track of seasonal activities and record important

The temple at Chichén Itzá at the equinox, the sun illuminating the stairs

historical events, the most likely explanation is that they were devised for religious purposes. They were used to venerate the gods who first brought calendars to earth from the heavens.[28]

Maya calendars, astrology, and mythology were integrated into a single compelling system of belief. The Maya observed the sky and used calendars to predict solar and lunar eclipses, the cycles of the planet Venus, and the movements of the constellations. These were not mere mechanical occurrences, but were considered the activities of the gods, the actual recapitulation of mythical events from the time of creation.[29]

The repeating series of creations and destructions of the world described in the creation story was a reminder of the consequences of neglecting obligations to the gods, who make humanity's continued existence possible. The journey of the Hero Twins and their father through the

Underworld is played out every year by the annual procession of the constellations as they move across the Milky Way. This suggests that the movement of the stars and planets may have served as a basic structural model for the development of Maya mythology.[30]

THE MAYA CALENDAR

The Maya calendar was based on two cycles — the Sacred Round and the Vague Year. The Sacred Round of 260 days is made up of two smaller cycles: the numbers 1 through 13, and twenty different day names. Each day name represented a god, whose burden it was to carry time across the sky, marking the passage of night and day. The Vague Year of 365 days is similar to our modern solar year, and consists of 18 months of 20 days each, with a 5-day unlucky period at the end. The Maya considered this an ominous time that could precipitate danger and death. Linking these two calendars resulted in a larger cycle of 18,980 days — about 52 solar years. This so-called Calendar Round gave each day two names and numbers derived from both the Sacred Round and the Vague Year.[31] Archaeologists have found both of these solar calendars carved in stone dating as far back as 400 B.C., and they were likely in use long before.[32]

The 52-year cycle was inadequate in measuring the continual passage of time through the ages, however, so another calendar called the Long Count was added, which began on the day of creation (13 August 3114 B.C.). Based on a 20-day count called a *uinal*, it likely originated from the total number of fingers and toes on a human being (the Maya word for human being is *uinic*). The 360-day count was called a *tun*, the 7,200-day count, a *katun*, and the 144,000-day count, a *baktun*. A single day was known as a *kin*.

Maya calendars were extremely accurate and precise. One of the important functions of the system was not to fix dates accurately in time, but to correlate the actions of Maya rulers to historic and mythological events. The acts of gods performed in the distant myth time were reenacted by their rulers, often on the anniversary of the original performance. Calendars were also used to mark the time of past and future happenings. For example, some Maya monuments record the dates of events that took place 90 million years ago, while others predict what will take place 3,000 years in the future.[33]

Of all the calendar cycles, it was the 260-day ritual calendar or Sacred Round that was used to determine important activities related to the gods. It named individuals, dictated when battles should be fought and individuals should marry, and provided the framework for Maya writings. Early texts speak of the prowess of chiefs and rulers, their involvement in historic events, and their genealogical links to important ancestors and supernatural forces.

A   **B**

1   2   3   4   5

The final text and picture of the eclipse table from the Dresden Codex. The figure at the bottom represents Venus; the two circular shapes above the feet represent the eclipse of the sun and the moon.

Drawing by Michael Closs

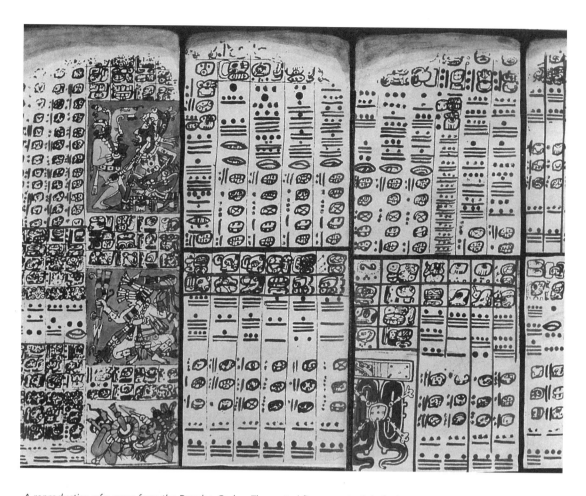

A reproduction of a page from the Dresden Codex. The central figure on the left depicts Venus as a warrior. This scene prophesies drought and implores farmers to pray to the Rain Gods.

MAYA WRITING

The Maya writing system is considered the most sophisticated ever developed in Mesoamerica. The Maya used individual signs or hieroglyphics, shown singularly or in elaborate versions featuring profiles of heads or full figures of people, animals, or gods. The glyphs stood for words or syllables that could be combined into any word in the Maya language — numbers and time periods, royal names and titles, kinship terms and events, and the names of gods, scribes, sculptors, objects, buildings, places, and even food.[34] Inscriptions were carved on stone and wood, and painted on paper, walls, and pottery.

Maya codices were made from deer hides or bark paper covered with a thin layer of plaster and folded like a screen. The inscriptions were painted by highly trained scribes. Most of the books have been lost because they were burned by the Spanish during the sixteenth century in their attempts to convert the Maya to Roman Catholicism. The few surviving books are an invaluable source of information about Maya religious beliefs and the calendar cycle of ritual celebrations. In picture form and in glyphs, they record information about the gods associated with each day as well as astronomical tables anticipating the cycles of Venus and eclipses of the sun.

The Maya had no alphabet. Instead, they used individual signs and images arranged in columns. Texts included a minimum of three or four glyphs and sometimes as many as fifty. During the Classic period, Maya texts were paired in columns that read together from left to right and from top to bottom.

Only a small segment of society controlled the knowledge of writing and reading. Writing, considered a sacred gift from the gods, was jealously guarded by the elite. They believed that it was their job to mediate between commoners and the "givers of knowledge."[35]

From the very beginning, the Maya used writing for propaganda rather than as a tool for recording accurate historical details. Inscriptions on stone monuments were designed to place kings in the most favourable light possible. In a hierarchical society where the elite competed for prestige and leadership positions, writing reinforced a ruler's military might and legitimized his descent from noble ancestors and mythical beings.[36]

The Maya hieroglyphic signs were first catalogued in 1962. Since 1980, there has been a great deal of progress in deciphering many new glyphs from Palenque, Tikal, and other sites. Although caution is advised in interpreting these writings because of their self-serving nature, the ongoing work of decoding the glyphs holds promise that many of the mysteries surrounding the Maya may one day be solved.

MAYA MATHEMATICS

The Maya used a counting system that required only three symbols to add, subtract, and keep track of days that stretched incredible distances into the past and future. A dot had a numerical value of one, a bar a value of five, and zero was represented by a stylized shell. That they understood the value of zero was remarkable, since most of the world's civilizations had no notion of this concept. Their mathematics also depended on place-value numeration, that is, the idea that the position of a number determined its value.

Here is how their system worked. Ten is represented by two bars, one on top of the other; nineteen is three bars with four dots on top. For numbers greater than nineteen, they used the same sequence of glyphs but placed a dot above the number for each group of twenty. For example, thirty-two consisted of the symbol for twelve with a dot on top representing an additional group of twenty. This kind of counting system could extend ad infinitum.

The system of dots, bars, and shells allowed even uneducated people to do the simple arith-

Mathematician with the numbers (starting at his arm pit) 13 and 1 through 9 written on his scarf
Drawing by Michael Closs

metic needed for trade and commerce. They took the two numbers to be added, placed them side by side, then collapsed them into a sum. They did the opposite for subtraction. Multiplication was more complicated, but still possible without formal education or the use of tables.[37] The value of money was probably fixed by the kings and their courts. Precious commodities such as greenstone beads, beads of red spiny oyster shells, cacao beans, lengths of cotton cloth, and quantities of sea salt were used for currency.[38]

Each day on the 260-day calendar had a number with various associations that could be good, bad, or neutral. It was the task of diviners to select a particular association out of the range of possibilities to determine the correct meaning of the calendar numbers and help individuals make important decisions about their work and personal lives.[39] The Sacred Round greatly influenced the daily lives of both nobles and commoners. Destinies were affected by birthdates and other significant dates that were examined to find out, for example, when and whom one should marry, the best day to begin planting maize, or when a ruler should lead his forces into battle.

The 365-day Maya Calendar

The first eighteen hieroglyphs represent the eighteen 20-day months that make up the Maya calendar year; the nineteenth hieroglyph symbolizes the last five unlucky days at the end of the year.

Conclusion

Today, many Maya-speaking people continue to follow in the footsteps of their ancestors. Although circumstances have changed, religious beliefs are vitally important in determining their concept of reality. Those who follow ancient customs still communicate with the dead by descending into deep underground caves; they pray to Chac, the Rain God, around a raised altar that symbolizes the First Mountain; they conduct sacrificial rituals in honour of their covenant with the gods. As we have seen throughout their history, the creation story has had a significant influence on how Maya perceive the world and their responsibility to their gods.

Although the Maya civilization has evolved in a unique manner, universal truths embodied in their beliefs are echoed in many of the world's great religions. Modern psychologists and anthropologists have looked at creation myths from different cultures and found many cross-cultural connections. Myths have been described as the collective dreams of society, which create archetypes or patterns that profoundly affect attitudes and behaviour. By giving us insight into the human psyche, myths allow us to gain a better understanding of ourselves as well as the dynamics at work within the community at large.

One of the archetypal patterns of the Maya worldview is the concept of a three-tiered universe. Psychologists suggest that this notion mirrors the struggle in the human psyche to find balance. The Underworld represents the subconscious mind or shadow side; the Upper World, a striving for greater awareness. The Middle World, the body, is the place where these two forces interact, creating the energy that propels life. This reflects a basic scientific truth: opposites attract and unite two opposing forces. As the Maya sought help from their ancestors in the Underworld and built temples to lift them closer to the gods in the Upper World, they were symbolically reaching for higher consciousness. The quest for higher knowledge and unity is a universal theme — the search for meaning by striving for something greater than ourselves.

An ancestor emerging from the mouth of a vision serpent. The serpent rises out of a bowl containing blood-stained paper.

The resurrection of the Maize God, Hun Hunahpu, out of the earth (symbolized by a turtle). His sons, the Hero Twins, assist.

The Hero Twins' search for their dead father and uncle in the Underworld is a common motif found in myths around the world. This Orpheus-like tale of a hero's journey to recover the beloved's soul can be symbolically understood as the search for the inner self. By struggling against fears that loom up from the depths of the unconscious, a person can develop the strength to face new challenges.

Another theme in the evolution of Maya culture is the rise and fall of kingship. The idea that humans are made in the image of the Creator and that monarchs have a direct connection to the spirit world are concepts found in many cultures. The role of kings and leaders in setting an example for society to follow is still alive in the modern mind. People continue to look to monarchs, elected officials, and religious and community leaders, expecting them to be above reproach. When their faults and shortcomings come to light, society suffers. The Maya gave up the monarchy over a thousand years ago. Perhaps they realized that commoners as well as kings could reach for the stars and communicate with the gods.

The Maya culture is still alive and vibrant. Enriching all those who come in contact with it, it has shown incredible resilience in adapting to change without losing its integrity. We can learn many lessons from the Maya. As communities struggle to maintain their identities, opposing forces are at work moving towards cultural homogenization. The challenge will be to find ways to respect differences, even as international trade and electronic communications make the global village smaller day by day.

Appendix A

The Maya Pantheon[40]

THE FIRST MOTHER AND FIRST FATHER

The First Mother, the Moon Goddess, was born six years before the first Father, Hun Nal Ye. Also known as the Maize God and the Plumed or Feathered Serpent, the First Father was responsible for overseeing the new creation of the cosmos. He was born on creation day, when he entered the sky and raised up the first Great Tree, upon which he landed. In so doing, he created a cosmic house located at the Polaris, the North Star, where the crown of the Great Tree stood. In Mesoamerica, the North Star is seen low on the horizon, giving the illusion that the entire cosmos pivots around this star.[41] The First Mother and First Father are the Creator Couple described in the *Popol Vuh*. All the other gods who subsequently came into being were the offspring of this couple.

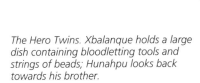

The Hero Twins. Xbalanque holds a large dish containing bloodletting tools and strings of beads; Hunahpu looks back towards his brother.

HUNAHPU AND XBALANQUE: THE HERO TWINS

These Maya culture heroes overcame the forces of death, paving the way for the conception of humans. They are usually shown wearing red and white cloth headbands, a symbol of Maya rulership. The face of Hunahpu serves as a glyph for the day name *ahau*, meaning king. He is often depicted with large black spots on his cheeks and body. Xbalanque can be identified by the jaguar-skin patches around his mouth and on his torso and limbs.[42]

39

THE PATRONS OF WRITING

The Hero Twins had two older brothers who were jealous of the twins and did everything they could to make to make their younger brothers' lives difficult. Their father, Hun Hunahpu, is sometimes depicted as an artist, as are his two older sons. The Hero Twins changed their brothers into monkeys and they became the patron gods of scribes.[43] They appear as monkey-men wielding pens and ink pots made from shells.

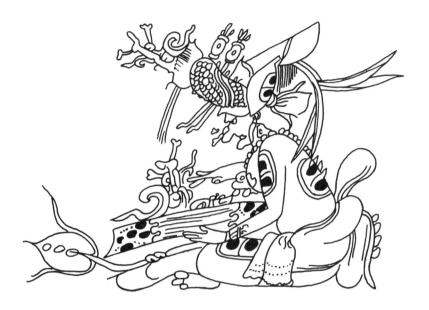

Monkey God writing in a codex decorated with jaguar skins

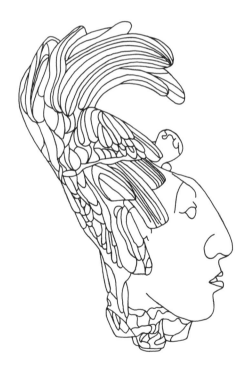

This stucco head of Pacal was found beneath his sarcophagus. His hairstyle and sloping nose imitate the classic features of the Maize God.

THE MAIZE GOD

The Maize God is depicted as a handsome youth with maize leaves and an ear of corn sprouting from his head. The flattened and elongated forehead of this deity is often accentuated by a partly shaven head and eyebrows, leaving patches of hair on the top of his head, which resembles a ripened ear of corn. The removal of the corn from the stalk at harvest represents his decapitation, the same fate Hun Hunahpu (the Hero Twins' father) met when he was killed by the Lords of Death in the creation story.[44] Like the Sun God, the Maize God is associated with life and death. He follows the path across the sky, descends into the Underworld, is reborn, and returns to the Sky World.

The Maya elite practised changing the shape of their offsprings' skulls to resemble the Maize God's elongated head by tying two boards front and back against the infant's head. Since a baby's skull bones are thin and pliable, the skull became long and pointed, giving the forehead its distinctive sloping profile. This practice caused much pain, and some infants died from complications such as infections and a disrupted blood supply.

ITZAM-YEH:
THE CELESTIAL BIRD

Also known as the Serpent Bird and Seven Macaw, Itzam-Yeh is associated with the four corners of the world as described in the creation story. He also marked the four corners of the temple, thereby establishing the sacred mountain's summit. The platform on temples where kings performed rituals is a re-creation of the original mountain platform. This bird pretended to be the sun when he landed on the Great Tree and was shot down with a blowgun by one of the Hero Twins. The royal headdresses made from the long, brilliant green feathers of the quetzal bird are symbolic representations of Itzam-Yeh.

The Celestial Bird
Drawing by Linda Schele

ITZAMNÁ:
LORD OF THE HEAVENS

Itzamná, or "Lizard House," is a high-ranking god who was the first shaman and diviner. He was associated with the Maya elite , who considered him an ancient form of the omnipotent, supreme deity. The word *itz* can mean shaman, a person who could open the portals to the spirit world. Maya kings and shamans contact Itzamná to plead with him to open the way so sacred nourishment will flow into the world to sustain humanity.[45] This god is also the inventor of writing and the patron of learning and the sciences. Often pictured in association with a double-headed serpent, he is also drawn as a man with large square eyes, an overhanging nose, a toothless mouth, and wearing a headband decorated with a hanging flower.

Itzamná

41

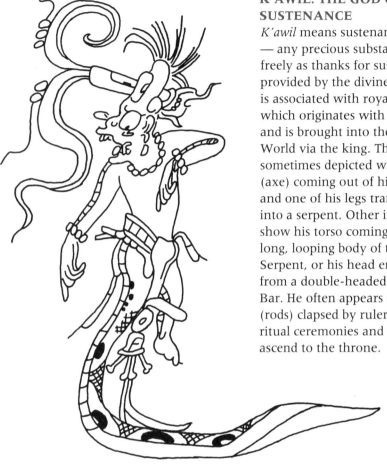

K'awil God

K'AWIL: THE GOD OF SUSTENANCE

K'awil means sustenance or alms — any precious substance given freely as thanks for sustenance provided by the divine.[46] K'awil is associated with royal power, which originates with the gods and is brought into the Middle World via the king. This deity is sometimes depicted with a celt (axe) coming out of his forehead and one of his legs transformed into a serpent. Other images show his torso coming out of the long, looping body of the Vision Serpent, or his head emerging from a double-headed Serpent Bar. He often appears on sceptres (rods) clapsed by rulers during ritual ceremonies and when they ascend to the throne.

IX CHEL: LADY RAINBOW

Ix Chel is wife to the high god, Itzamná. She oversees weaving, medicine, and childbirth. Like the First Mother, she is a moon goddess, who is depicted sitting in a moon sign holding a rabbit. In the Maya codices, she appears as an aged, toothless woman; her head functions as the numeral "one" and the phonetic "na."

Ix Chel

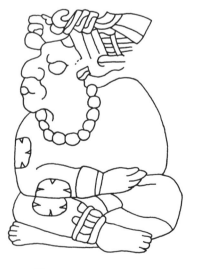

The Jaguar Sun God

THE JAGUAR SUN GOD

Almighty God the Sun dwells in the highest levels of heaven.[47] When he traces the path of the sun across the sky in the day-time, his name is Kinich Ahau. When the sun falls into the West Door and enters the Underworld, he becomes the fearsome Jaguar God. The circular path the sun takes across the sky and into the Underworld is the Great Round, symbolically represented by a snake chasing its tail.

CHAC: THE RAIN GOD AND COSMIC MONSTER

In the creation story, Chacs were placed at the four corners of the world. They bring the rains by shedding their blood; they create thunderbolts by hurling down their stone axes. Rain is depicted as great scrolls of blood flowing from their mouths and stingray spines. The blood shed by these gods is the supernatural counterpoint to the blood shed by royalty in ritual sacrifices as a means of providing sustenance for the gods.[48]

Chac is a dragon-like monster with a crocodilian head and deer ears. His legs usually terminate in deer hooves with water-blood scrolls at the joints. As he exists on the perimeter of the cosmos, this cosmic monster marks the path between the natural and supernatural worlds.[49] He is sometimes depicted with two heads, one representing the sun, and the other, Venus. In the night sky, Chac's arching reptilian body can be seen stretching across the Milky Way.

Chac, the Rain God

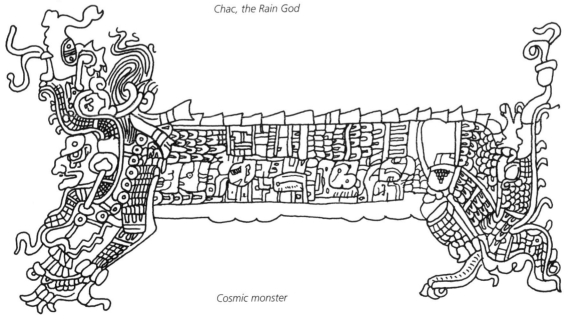

Cosmic monster

43

The Witz monster

THE WITZ MONSTER

The Witz monster is the symbol of the living mountain. He is depicted with a zoomorphic face, a huge gaping mouth, and a stepped cleft in the centre of his forehead. Images of this creature were placed on temples to transform them into sacred, living mountains. The open mouth became the entry into the mountain, symbolizing both the doorway to a temple and the mouth of a cave. Today, as in the past, people still search for water in caves and *cenotes* and perform rituals in these sacred places. The Maya believe these openings in the earth are passageways to the Underworld, where their ancestors and the Lords of the Dead reside.

THE LORDS OF DEATH

Many Maya gods dwell in the Underworld, the dreaded Xibalbá. The Lords of Death are depicted as skeleton people or ugly bloated beings wearing ornaments such as disembodied eyes taken from the dead. The Maya believe that when people die, they enter the Underworld through a cave or a *cenote*. When kings died, they followed the path linked to the cosmic movement of the sun and fell into the Underworld, but because they possessed supernatural powers, they were reborn into the Sky World and became gods.[50]

Death God

Appendix B

Synopsis of the Film
Mystery of the Maya

Mystery of the Maya is an exciting archaeological journey through Maya history. A young Maya boy who lives close to the ruins begins to wonder about the people who built these amazing structures. He becomes acquainted with one of the archaeologists (portrayed in the film by the Mexican actress Blanca Guerra) and asks her to tell him about his ancestors. This sets the stage to explore the ancient sites and to discover how the story of this civilization is being revealed.

The crew travelled to over fifteen locations in Mexico and Guatemala to create this giant-screen motion picture, which includes aerial views of Maya ruins and key events in modern Mexican archaeology. The film begins with a view of Tulum, located by the Caribbean Sea on the Yucatán Peninsula, moves on to Palenque, site of the magnificent Temple of the Inscriptions, to Chichén Itzá's famous "Castillo" temple and other well-known sites on *la ruta Maya*.

Dramatizations illustrate scenes from traditional Maya life, the period of the Spanish invasion, and contemporary events such as a prayer ritual deep within a cave. Descendants of the ancient Maya pray to the same gods their ancestors worshipped a hundred generations ago. The discovery of the secret staircase that led to the tomb of the seventh-century ruler of Palenque, King Pacal, is reenacted, as is the work of the nineteenth-century explorers who first documented the existence of Maya cities.

You will feel part of the historic expeditions (1839–42) led by John Lloyd Stephens, an American writer of popular travel books, and his companion, the English artist Frederick Catherwood, as they venture into the jungle on

Snake image and weaving patterns sculpted on the Nunnery, a group of buildings at Uxmal

The artist Frederick Catherwood making accurate drawings of stone carvings (reenactment scene from the IMAX® film)

the trail of a "lost" civilization. Catherwood's accurate drawings in Stephens's *Incidents of Travel in Central America, Chiapas, and Yucatán* (1841) are an invaluable record of many stone carvings that have since been damaged or lost. This book provided the first opportunity for the world to ponder the achievements of the Maya civilization and to speculate on the reasons for its demise.

A wealthy Englishman, Alfred Maudslay, visited the area forty years later. Using a scientific approach, he surveyed as many sites as possible, producing accurate records of the architecture, carvings, and hieroglyphics. Capitalizing on improvements in photographic technology (such as the invention of the dry-plate gelatin negative, which allowed photographers to work away from their studios), he took hundreds of photographs

of various sites. Some of this rich photographic legacy is shown in the film, as fresh today as when the images were created. In addition, Maudslay made plaster moulds of the glyphs and images that he had recorded on film.

The film also relives an important chapter in Maya history. In 1562, the Franciscan bishop Diego de Landa decided to burn all the Maya books he could find in a massive public bonfire because he felt they contained nothing but "superstitions and the writings of the devil." This act obliterated most of the information the Maya had recorded on their history and sciences. Today only four fragmentary books survive: in Dresden, Paris, Madrid, and Mexico City. Ironically, although he destroyed this treasury of knowledge, it is through Landa's own writings that we know as

A nobleman wearing a feather headdress, shell earrings, and body paint (reenactment scene from the IMAX® film)

much as we do of Maya customs, clothing, and lifestyle. His attempts to decipher Maya hieroglyphics ultimately contributed to their translation by modern scholars.

Another reenactment in the film recounts the story of the spectacular Bonampak murals. In 1946, the American United Fruit Company hired the photographer Giles Healey to document the ancient traditions of the Lacondón Maya. He persuaded a few local men to take him to temples in remote parts of the jungle, some of which had never been seen by non-Natives, where he witnessed traditional ceremonies that demonstrated the continuity of Maya culture. He was also led to the Temple of Three Rooms at Bonampak, where he became the first non-Maya to gaze on the exceptional wall frescos showing Maya kings in full regalia and performing various rituals including torture.

The film also considers some remarkable Maya achievements. Their system of mathematics and calendrics, for example, was highly advanced and extremely accurate. Maya writing effectively recorded historical events as well as ideas associated with their religious beliefs and practices. In addition, the Maya were expert astronomers who measured planetary cycles and predicted solar and lunar eclipses.

Animation sequences focus on the deciphering of the famous "96 glyphs" from Palenque and demonstrate the work of numerous scholars as the puzzle of various glyphs was worked out. It was not until 1990 that the meaning of the full panel of glyphs became clear. They read like a history book, describing royal families, exploits of war, and the ascension of young kings to the throne. The monument of one of those kings,

"Shield Jaguar" accepting a water-lily helmet from his principal wife, Lady Xoc (reenactment scene from the IMAX® film)

Lord Pacal, is featured in the film. The limestone sarcophagus lid of his tomb, engraved with a superb example of Maya art, is considered a world treasure.

The film ends with some insights about the unsolved mystery of why so many cities were abandoned at the end of the Classic period (around A.D. 900). Why did the Maya give up their kings and return to a simple lifestyle as farmers of maize — the cornerstone of their civilization for over a millennium?

Mystery of the Maya is a breathtaking film filled with the vastness and grandeur of ancient cities as well as the exotic sights and sounds of the region's spectacular natural beauty. It was co-produced by the National Film Board of Canada, the Instituto Mexicano de Cinematografía, and the Canadian Museum of Civilization, in association with Mexico's Secretaría de Turismo and Consejo Nacional para la Cultura y las artes.

Notes

1. Lawana Hooper-Trout, *The Maya* (New York: Chelsea House, 1991), 14-18.

2. Linda Schele and David Freidel, *A Forest of Kings: The Untold Story of the Ancient Maya* (New York: William Morrow, 1990), 56.

3. Ibid., 142.

4. Michael D. Coe, *The Maya*, 5th ed., rev. and exp. (London: Thames and Hudson, 1993), 40.

5. Schele, *Forest*, 72.

6. Unless otherwise stated, the sections on the Preclassic and Classic periods, The First Kings, and Expanding the Cornfields are based on Schele, *Forest*, 56-59.

7. Coe, *The Maya*, 17.

8. Hooper-Trout, *The Maya*, 27.

9. Ibid., 47.

10. Schele, *Forest*, 379-80.

11. This version of the *Popol Vuh* and the section Maize Dough and the Three Stones are based on David Freidel, Linda Schele, and Joy Parker, *Maya Cosmos: Three Thousand Years on the Shaman's Path* (New York: William Morrow, 1993), 107-13.

12. Ibid., 65.

13. Ibid., 61.

14. Schele, *Forest*, 429, n34.

15. Gene S. Stuart and George E. Stuart, *Lost Kingdoms of the Maya* (Washington, D.C.: National Geographic, 1993), 46.

16. Freidel, *Maya Cosmos*, 194.

17. Ibid., 108-10.

18. Karl Taube, *Aztec and Maya Myths* (London: British Museum Press; Austin: University of Texas Press, 1993), 62.

19. Freidel, *Maya Cosmos*, 194-95.

20. Schele, *Forest*, 66-67.

21. Freidel, *Maya Cosmos*, 137.

22. Ibid., 142-43.

23. Ibid., 204-7.

24. Ibid., 257-59.

25. Ibid., 343.

26. This section is based on Schele, *Forest*, 221-26.

27. Ibid., 68-69.

28. Zecharia Sitchin, *The Lost Realms* (New York: Avon Books, 1990), 155-56.

29. Taube, *Aztec*, 15.

30. Ibid., 75-76.

31. Stuart, *Lost Kingdoms*, 176-77.

32. Joyce Marcus, *Mesoamerican Writing Systems: Propaganda, Myth, and History in Four Ancient Civilizations* (Princeton: Princeton University Press, 1992), 42.

33. Ibid., 14.

34. Stuart, *Lost Kingdoms*, 158.

35. Marcus, *Mesoamerican Writing*, 28.

36. Ibid., 15-16.

37. Schele, *Forest*, 433.

38. Ibid., 92.

39. Marcus, *Mesoamerican Writing*, 96-97.

40. Freidel, *Maya Cosmos*. Unless otherwise stated, the information on the Maya pantheon comes from pages 407-18.

41. Ibid., 69-75.

42. Taube, *Aztec*, 64.

43. Ibid.

44. Ibid., 63.

45. Freidel, *Maya Cosmos*, 51.

46. Ibid., 194.

47. Ibid., 128.

48. Schele, *Forest*, 66.

49. Ibid., 70.

50. Hooper-Trout, *The Maya*, 54-59.